To

_____

From

_____

Date

_____

A Love that Lasts Forever

GARY SMALLEY

WORD PUBLISHING

NASHVILLE

A Thomas Nelson Company

To my daughter, Kari,

and daughters-in-law, Erin and Amy,

with special thanks for

loving me and making my life so much fun.

My love for you will last forever.

Contents

A Love That Lasts Forever

"Gary," he asked, "do you love Norma?"

"Well . . . yes," I said. (Norma was sitting right beside me . . . what else could I say?!) But now I realize that I really didn't understand what it meant to truly love her in the way the Scriptures describe.

Then the pastor asked me a second question, "Gary, would you lay down your life for her?"

Again I said yes, thinking he was asking if I would throw myself in front of a truck for her, or step in front of a gunman to take the bullet meant for her.

The truth of the matter is, when I married Norma I knew the right words—but not the right answers. I didn't have a plan to go by, and after marrying a sparky, enthusiastic, godly woman, it took me about five years of applying the wrong information regarding relationships to knock the sparkle right out of her life.

Early in our marriage, I could tell we weren't doing well, so I decided to try a few quick-fix remedies. I tried the "If you'd just change" tactic, and even resorted to the lecture method of teaching her what the Scriptures say about being a godly wife. I never used an overhead

A love that lasts thrives on shared,

minor crises that, when remembered,

prompt laughter.

projector, but I probably would have if I'd thought about it. Many a night, 99 percent of our dinner table conversations were actually my lectures aimed at drilling into Norma what the Bible said she should do to make "us" happy.

During all that time, I conveniently ignored the scriptural words of wisdom that applied to the husband—probably because I had never taken the time to truly understand the concepts behind the words. And to go one step deeper, without realizing it, I was covering up my own weaknesses and feelings of inadequacy by pointing out hers.

Norma kept hoping that I'd "get with it," but I never did. As she saw her hopes for a warm, fulfilling family life slipping away, she felt resigned to a marriage that would never match her dreams.

After nearly five years of watching our relationship grow more and more strained, I came home one day, walked into the kitchen, and greeted Norma with the usual, "Hi, I'm home." But she didn't respond.

"Is anything wrong?" I asked.

I knew from the look on her face and her nonverbal expressions that I didn't need to ask the question. It was obvious that something was drastically "wrong."

Suddenly I felt tired all over. I had been battling my conscience for years and spent untold energy to keep up a facade of closeness to those at the church. Here I was teaching and counseling each week on relationships, and in my own marriage I felt like a failure. After years of pretending, I knew I didn't need a quick "self-help" gimmick to get through to my wife. I needed the kind of total heart transplant that only God can give. And so I gently put

my arm around her and asked, "Norma, what do you think is wrong in our relationship?"

"Oh, no, you don't," Norma said, pulling back from me, her eyes filling with tears.

"You're not going to get me to share what I'm feeling and then turn it into another lecture on what I'm doing wrong."

"Honey," I said, trying to stay as soft as I could, "I can see how you'd feel that way, and I'm very, very sorry, but could you please just tell me one more time? I promise you, this time you won't hear a lecture."

Reluctantly Norma did share with me the concerns that had been building up in her heart, and while it may have been her one-hundredth time to tell me, I had never heard it the way she explained it that day. Little did I know that this single conversation would become one of the most traumatic—yet one of the most significant—moments in our lives.

It was the beginning of dramatic change in our marriage and the foundation of many more lessons to come on how to have a love that lasts forever.

You may be newly in love, engaged, newly married, married a short time, or celebrating your fiftieth wedding anniversary—wherever you are, and whoever you are, I know something about you. You want a love relationship with your husband or wife that will not only last forever, but will also grow stronger and deeper and more satisfying over the years ahead. In this book we'll draw a picture of what a love that will stand the test of time looks like, as well as offer ideas and insights that will help you create the kind of marriage you really want.

We'll start by going back to that afternoon so long ago. Norma said several important things that afternoon, but there was one thing in particular I'll never forget. Read on. . . .

Invites Honor as a Permanent Resident

ary, I feel like everything on this earth is far more important to you than I am.

"I feel that all the football games you watch on television are more important than I am, the newspaper, your hobbies, your counseling at the church. Gary, I can spend hours working in the kitchen, and you never say a word. I can even farm out the kids to a baby-sitter and have a candlelight dinner all prepared for you, and the phone will ring and you'll say, 'Oh, I'm not doing anything important. I'm just eating. Sure, I'll be right over.' Then you're gone, telling me to keep something warm for you in the oven.

"It's like I don't matter to you, but other people do. In fact, sometimes I feel that you're more polite to total strangers than you are to me. You'll say the most awful things to me, but never to anyone else, especially not people at the church. . . ."

She went on, but you get the point—and so did I. While it may have been a message that was on continuous play around our house, I was hearing the recording loud and clear for the first time.

A love that lasts forever highly values

each other, daily giving the other

a place of prominence in each one's life.

Before talking with Norma, I would never have stood up in front of a group and said that my counseling or even the nonstop sporting events I watched on television were more important than my wife, but without realizing it, that's exactly what I was communicating to her.

Little did I know that for five years of marriage, I had also been violating a crucial biblical concept that lies at the heart of any strong relationship. Every time I ignored its power to build loving, lasting relationships, I was literally shutting the door to the kind of home and family I'd wanted all my life.

What is this biblical principle that I'd been ignoring for years—and that weakened my marriage as a result? It's a simple, yet incredibly powerful, principle, and it comes wrapped in a single word—*honor.*

THE TRUE MEANING OF HONOR

During biblical times, the word *honor* carried a literal meaning that has been all but lost by translation and time. For a Greek living in Christ's day, something of "honor" called to mind something "heavy, or weighty." Gold, for example, was the perfect picture of something of "honor," because it was heavy and valuable at the same time.

For this same Greek, the word *dishonor* would also bring to mind a literal picture. The word for "dishonor" actually meant "mist" or "steam." Why? Because the lightest, most insignificant thing the Greeks could think of was the steam rising off a pot of boiling water, or clouding a mirror on a cold winter day.

When we honor particular people we're saying in effect that who they are and what they say carry great weight with us. They're extremely valuable in our eyes. Just the opposite is true when we dishonor them. In effect, by our verbal or nonverbal statements, we're saying that their words or actions make them of little value or "lightweights" in our eyes.

BRINGING HONOR INTO YOUR HOME

I have to admit that at the time, I didn't know exactly what it meant to put the concept of honor into action in our home, but I knew enough to realize that honor would have to be a daily—sometimes hourly—decision. And I had made that decision. I wasn't going to keep Norma on a starvation diet of praise and three full meals of criticism and unrealistic expectations anymore. I was going to consistently feed her a nourishing meal of significance and high value in our home.

"Norma," I said, "I know you have every reason to doubt me, but I mean what I'm saying. I never understood this before, and I want to ask you to forgive me for making you think that everything else I'm doing is more important than you. No matter how I've acted in the past, that's not what I really believe."

Our evening discussion was over, and she wasn't dazzled by my promise of change. In fact, because of the five years she had lived with the "old Gary," it took her almost two full years of a consistent track record of honoring acts to finally believe the "new Gary" was for real.

Norma has never failed to forgive me when I asked her, and she forgave me that day. But she was right to question whether I would actually follow through on my promises. She'd been standing in fifth or sixth place in my life for so long, it was natural for her to be skeptical. It was hard for her to believe she was finally moving to the front of the line.

With honor as a permanent resident in a home, there is hope to restore relationships with God and loved ones. Feelings that have taken years to develop don't change overnight, but persistent honor has the power to win over even the hardest of hearts—particularly as a husband or wife sees affirming actions become a consistent part of a marriage.

The most effective way to open the door to needed changes in a relationship is to honor a loved one. And once we've made that decision to honor, love is the action we take no matter how we feel. Genuine love is honor put into action, regardless of the cost. It comes from a heart overflowing with affection for God, freeing us to seek another person's best interest.

Taps into a Woman's Built-In Marriage Manual

t was a wise and loving God who said, "It is not good for the man to be alone" (Genesis 2:18a). But was a woman designed merely to provide a man with companionship—or does it go deeper than that?

Most people are familiar with the passage that talks about God creating woman and His words, "I will make [Adam] a helper suitable for him" (Genesis 2:18b). The Hebrew word for "helper" actually means "complete." The word is used throughout the Old Testament to talk about God being our "helper," the One who "completes what is lacking," or "does for us what we cannot do for ourselves."

In other words, a wife is designed to bring strengths to the relationship that the husband does not naturally have himself.

Do you know the main reason why men are held back from a promotion at work? Is it a lack of technical skill? Rarely. A lack of education? Occasionally. But the primary reason men fail to be promoted is their lack of relationship skills.

What most men don't realize is that they have the world's greatest instructors in

A love that lasts forever

is courageous enough to ask,

"What would make this

relationship better?"

relationship skills living right under their roofs. A wife is a gold mine of relational skills. If a man wants to take advantage of the "missing part" of the nature that has affected every "Adam" since the beginning, all he has to do is look into the eyes of his wife and learn to tap into her built-in marriage manual.

So here's how a husband can tap into this rich source of relational skills to improve his own marriage—and his skills with his children and others as a result. First, a man needs to realize that his wife comes equipped with two tremendous inner strengths:

1. She has a strong, innate desire for a good and healthy relationship; and

2. She has the natural ability to recognize a great relationship.

TAP INTO A WOMAN'S BUILT-IN MARRIAGE MANUAL

Three simple but life-changing questions are all it takes. For the sake of argument, let's say Bob is going to ask Julie these questions:

Julie, I realize that one way God equipped you as a helper was to complete me in the relational side of life. So let's begin with our marriage . . .

Question #1: On a scale from one to ten, with one being terrible and ten being a great marriage, where would you like our relationship to be?

Naturally, almost every woman (and man, too!) answers that they'd like to consistently be around a nine or a ten. After all, how many of us are into misery? Bob would then go on to Question 2:

Question #2: On a scale from one to ten, overall, where would you rate our marriage today?

In most cases, a man will rate the marriage two to three points higher than his wife will, so don't let the initial difference in perception shock you. Remember, the average woman is much more in tune with the state of the relationship than the average man.

Be sure to give her time to think and share, and reassure her that you value her opinion and want to understand her as much as possible.

Whether you agree with your wife or not, it's important to honor her by giving her your full attention. The goal is to understand her and to be open to what she has to say.

The next question is the crucial one. In fact, in some ways it doesn't matter what she answers to Question 2, for the most important question is the third one—the one that can flip open the pages to her natural marriage and relationship manual.

Question #3: As you look at our relationship, what are some specific things we could do over the next six weeks that would move us closer to a ten?

I have yet to find a woman who cannot paint the answer to that question in brilliant detail. However, I have met numerous men who can't even find the paintbrush!

In some cases, your wife may be reluctant to answer this question, fearing she'll hurt your feelings—or even worse, that you'll hurt *her* feelings by your defensive response. That's why it's important to patiently give her the time to talk and to consistently reassure her about the security of your relationship—no matter what she says or where she rates things. If she feels secure in your love, almost without exception she'll be able to open up with many helpful specifics on how you can more effectively steward the gift of the marriage and family God has given you.

Let me state something clearly, however. Valuing his wife's differences, and even tapping into her built-in marriage manual, does not transfer leadership or responsibility away from the husband and place it onto the wife. Biblically, there is no escape clause for the man from being the head of the home—the man is the fact finder when it comes to building a strong relationship. But to be the type of loving leader God intended, allowing a wife to fulfill her God-given function as a loving "completer," is a must. It can help a man replace insensitivity with sensitivity and replace lording it over others with genuine love for them. It can also help men become the observant servant leaders they were always meant to be.

By appreciating the unique and wonderful way God has created a woman, we can add a richness and joy to our marriage that virtually everyone wants, but very few have. The secret is in learning to honor a woman as someone unmatched in God's creation, made especially by Him as a completer, to do things for a man he could never do for himself.

Unlocks a Man's Natural Strength for Loving Leadership

While it is true a man doesn't speak as many words or may not be as naturally sensitive as a woman, that doesn't mean he is incapable of being a great lover in the home. In fact, it seems that *God has built into every man the natural ability to be the very loving leader his family needs.*

Saying that God has designed a man to be the lover in a home may sound a bit strange with all we know about a man's conquering, logical, fact-driven nature, but that very nature is the foundation for my conviction.

Why? Because the kind of love that lasts, the kind that can grow and thrive apart from feelings, is the kind that comes from a decision. Love—stripped to its core—is just that, *a factual decision that doesn't have to depend on our feelings.*

When it comes to family relationships, that same hard-driving, conquering nature that can cause a man to get ahead in his profession, can cause one of two results at home. It can create emotional strain and tension if a man tries to blast through his family relationships

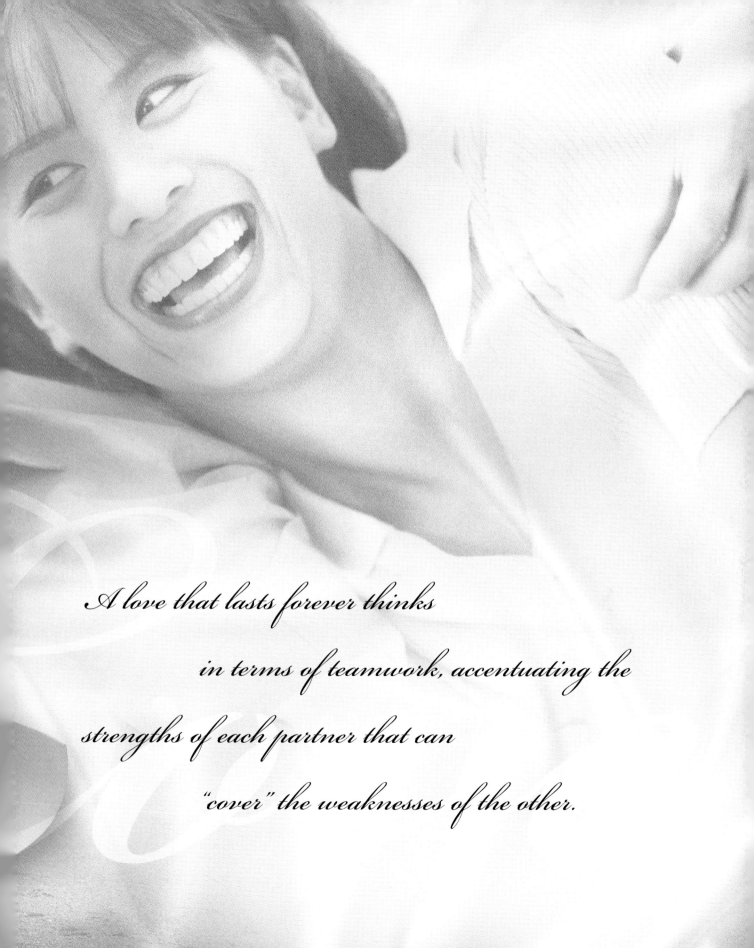

A love that lasts forever thinks

        in terms of teamwork, accentuating the

strengths of each partner that can

        "cover" the weaknesses of the other.

like so many projects at work, but take that same drive and harness it by giving a man a specific plan of action for the home—and it can be the driving force to bring about the very relationship a woman longs for.

Usually a man is not driven by an emotional need to relate. Rather, he'll be much more motivated to do something relational (like spending a half-hour in conversation) once he's made a factual decision that it's right. For a man, actions are primarily what dictate feelings, not the reverse.

In large part, I feel that a man's unique ability to blend fact and feeling is a major gift God has given him in order to carry out his responsibility of being the loving leader in a home. When a man is given the right information, told what is right to do and how to do it, he can draw on his natural force of will to make a decision that stays while his feelings may come and go.

A Biblical Blueprint
for Loving Leadership at Home

The first place a man should check to build a strong family is a blueprint found in Ephesians 5. In this important chapter, the man is called to be the "head" of his wife—the primary lover—just as Christ is the Head of the church and the lover of the church.

Nowhere does it say that a man is to "lord it over" his wife. In fact, Christ specifically commands that "lording it over" another person has no place in a Christian's relationships. Rather, the Scriptures tell me I am to love my wife as Jesus loves His church.

How did Christ lead in love? By serving, by committing Himself to our best interest, and by doing so regardless of the cost. The greatest among us are simply following a pattern Christ set down—namely, serving those He loved and for whom He laid down His life.

When it comes to "leadership" and headship in the home, one very specific guideline is found in verses 28–29: "Husbands ought to love their wives as their own bodies . . . (for) no one ever hated his own body, but he *feeds* and *cares* for it, just as Christ does the church" (emphasis added).

If we are following the biblical pattern for family leadership, we men are to nurture and cherish our wives (and children). We do so just as we nurture and cherish our own bodies—and as Christ nurtures and cherishes the church.

When a husband makes that first important decision to truly honor those entrusted to him, he takes the first step toward being the loving *nurturer* God meant him to be. As a result he can see his relationship begin to blossom before his eyes and grow.

GROWING A STRONG MARRIAGE

What does it mean to "nurture" one's wife?

The Greek word for "nurturer" means "husbandman." For those of us who haven't grown up on a farm, that's a tiller of the soil, a professional gardener. A nurturer is one who helps things grow, who provides a "greenhouse" atmosphere where the plants are shielded and protected.

In short, that's what I'm called to be as a husband. Like the top gardener at your local nursery, I am responsible for understanding what ingredients cause my marriage to grow and flower—and then for providing them on a consistent basis. My role as a "nurturer" is to be a fact finder. I should interview each member of my family with my fact-finder mind to see what needs should be met that day and then discover how best to meet them. When I do, I nurture, cover, and protect them—and get the privilege of watching them grow.

"Wait a minute," I can hear some men saying. "This nurturing business sounds like it puts all the responsibility on the man. What about the responsibility of the woman, or even the children, to make the home all it can be?"

Whenever I hear this argument, two things come to mind. First, it is true that a man is called to be the nurturer of his family, not a woman. In fact, the Scriptures never tell a woman to "love" her husband, but a man is specifically commanded to "love" his wife.

Throughout the Scriptures, a woman is pictured as the "responder" or reflector of her husband's and God's light. In the Song of Songs in the Old Testament, the bride of Solomon makes this important comment about their relationship, "Draw me after you and let us run together!" (1:4, NASB).

Can you see the balance in this perspective? The man initiates the loving actions (drawing her after him); the woman responds (let us run together); and then the two of them grow together as a result. A woman's natural calling is to be a completer, a helper, a responder to his love. In addition, she is called to honor her husband (Romans 12:10; 1 Peter 3:1). When it comes to who wears the nurturing shoes in the family, biblically they come in men's sizes.

"But how can I know specifically what my wife needs, so that her life and our marriage bloom and grow?" you may ask. "I barely have time to finish everything I've got going at work. How am I going to learn all it takes to care for her in the way I should? Isn't that asking a lot?"

You're exactly right. It is asking a great deal to see that a marriage becomes successful. Without a doubt, a husband has a high calling in taking on the role of the nurturer in a home, but the task isn't impossible. In fact, it's far from it. That is the tremendous value of a man, for God has given a man exactly what he needs to be a great lover and leader of his home.

Nurtures an Unconditional Commitment to an Imperfect Person

Every enduring marriage involves an unconditional commitment to an imperfect person. This means we can gaze at each other's imperfections and say, "Those things do irritate me, but I'm going to find out what caused them, and see if I can help. No matter what shape you're in—I'll be around to help you grow."

For all of us, security is an essential prerequisite, not an emotional elective. Let's be even more specific in discussing how we can help our loved ones grow by providing the sunlight of security for their lives. There are at least three things that every man and woman can begin to do to build a secure marriage on an everyday basis.

They can start by (1) building their own "hallway of honor" in their home, which in itself can help steer their mate or children away from the doorway of dishonor. Then they can (2) look to the Lord for the strength to make an unconditional commitment and sacrificial choices. Finally, (3) they can become students of their spouses' interests as a tangible way of expressing their commitment. All are important ways to build security in a home, but the

A love that lasts forever never

demands its own way but searches for

ways of enriching the other person.

first has a dual benefit. It not only builds positive things into the relationship, it can also help to keep tremendous pain from the people we care about most.

A Hallway of Honor

A marriage or family can't grow in a healthy way if security is constantly shifting in a home, but loved ones can live without perfection. In fact, the more genuine security a wife or child feels, the more they feel allowed to fail.

My family knows I'm not perfect; they know I'll lose my temper at times—and they know I'm not always as sensitive as I should be. But one thing that helps them be patient with my imperfections is the knowledge that I'm 100 percent committed to them. I "still want them to be my banker," and I'm trying hard to be the kind of father and husband I should be. With each act of commitment, they see me with hammer and nail, adding on to a hallway of honor in our home.

Perhaps for your spouse, security is a special event like a romantic dinner or going to a helpful marriage seminar. It may even be something as small as sending a card or calling home from the office each day just to see how your loved one is doing.

Norma has told me often that the way I "date" our kids makes her feel secure. I make it a practice to take my daughter, Kari, out on a special outing about once a month to show my commitment to Norma. The children are such an extension of her that simply knowing I am spending time with each child individually makes Norma feel secure in the strength and love I hold for our family.

A love that lasts forever relies on

God as its enduring source of power.

Again, like a wise gardener, ask your spouse, "What is security to you?" Then take careful notes of what he or she says. Security may be spelled, "Let me have a say in the financial decisions," or "Take the time to have family devotions," or "Call me each day when you have to travel."

If you understand what "security" means to them, then you can begin making deposit after deposit into their love bank. This accrues high interest in your relationship. Just begin with a few simple questions like, "On a one to ten scale, one being very 'insecure' and ten being very 'secure,' how confident do you feel in my love?" or "What could I specifically do over the next few months that would raise the level of security in our relationship?"

By seeking to build security into your spouse through small, positive acts, you do even more than add positive marks to the marital ledger. You also can help them (and yourself) to guard against the temptation to walk through a doorway named "dishonor."

The more security and honor we build into our homes—the tighter we help to shut the doorway to temptation for our loved ones. Interestingly, it also helps to shut tighter the door to temptation for ourselves.

There's a second way to develop security in a marriage that calls for the courage to make and keep an unconditional commitment to one's spouse. That commitment is often best seen in the sacrificial choices we may have to make if necessary.

SACRIFICIAL CHOICES

Betty waited in a little examination room in the doctor's office, her head lowered. Here it was, only two weeks before their only daughter's wedding, and she'd had another "lockup" with her arthritis.

Once Betty had been a cheerleader in the West Texas town in which she grew up. But you could never tell it now. Her heart and bubbly spirit were the same, but today (at fifty-five) they were trapped inside a body that was so crippled, she couldn't walk as well as most ninety-year-olds.

Betty was a brave woman, but as she sat in the privacy of the doctor's office, tears rolled down her cheeks. She thought of her marriage to Rusty and all their dreams. She remembered all the plans they'd made for their retirement years . . . that would always remain just dreams. She thought of all the places they wanted to travel . . . but now never could. In her heart she knew that her arms were so battered by arthritis she'd never even be able to hold her first grandchild—the pain would simply be too great.

The door to the room opened, and her husband walked in from talking with the doctor. Looking over at his wife, he could see her chin trembling as she fought to regain her composure.

Try as she might, she couldn't help breaking into sobs.

"Oh, Rusty, please leave me," she begged him. "I'm getting worse, not better. I'm a mess. It hurts too much for you to touch me. I'm spending every cent we've saved toward retirement fighting this thing. I'm a burden to you and the kids and you know it."

Her tall, weather-beaten husband pulled over a chair and sat down beside her. Gently he took her hand, twisted by arthritis, and said, "Sweetheart, it doesn't hurt to smile, does it? If you'll just smile at me now and then, that's all I need. I really don't even need that. I just need you."

Real love means a sacrificial, courageous commitment—especially when the other person may not be able to give back to you. Security should never be something you take on or off as you see fit. It's an abiding conviction that all is well with our commitment and all will be well—no matter what.

GOING BACK TO SCHOOL

Recently a close friend of ours, Jim Brawner, did a survey of several hundred teenagers. One of the first questions was: *"What is one tangible way your mother and/or father demonstrates that you're important to them?"* Can you guess what the number one response was, by far?

"I know they think I'm important because . . . they attend my games . . . my practices . . . my concerts . . . my open houses . . . my band competitions . . ." In other words, with a teenager, security can be spelled with three words, *"Come watch me!"*

While many men and women may not realize it, we never really outgrow the deep need we have for our loved ones to be excitedly supportive of our interests. What this means in a marriage is that the sunlight of security can shine on a marriage when we show an active interest in our loved one's life.

This was brought home to me in a tangible way when I first met a couple who became special friends. He was a huge offensive lineman for an NFL team when we first met, and his wife was perhaps 5'4" in heels. On the basis of size alone, there probably wasn't a more oddly matched pair. But in terms of their shared interests, the couple was only a heartbeat apart.

I met them at a Pro Athlete's Outreach Conference and was fascinated with a conversation we had at lunch one day. Out of curiosity, I asked this NFL wife how much she knew about the position her husband played on his team. I expected her to say something like, "Oh, he's paid to stand in front of other people." Instead, she gave me a ten-minute presentation on offensive blocking techniques.

Taken aback by her grasp of the sport, I asked how she'd become such an expert on her husband's position on the team. That's when she gave me a real-life lesson on what it means to become a spouse's biggest fan—by becoming a graduate student of their likes and dislikes.

She explained that when they were first married, she resented the time he spent on the practice field; she resented all the team meetings and the travel. Finally, she grew tired of feeling so negative all the time, and she decided to go on the offensive. She would stop

throwing spitballs from the back row, and get up in the front row and learn about his career that she resented so much.

She began to ask her husband all sorts of questions about playing on the line for a pro team. She even cornered a few of the assistant coaches to learn more intricate details of the game. The more she learned and read, the more of an encourager she became. That's when a funny thing happened.

As her level of encouragement and interest went up, she noticed their marriage improving. While it wasn't her goal to get anything from her husband in return, he began showing more than a passing interest in her likes and dislikes.

What this wise woman had done was to push back the dark clouds of resentment to let the sunlight of security shine on her marriage. She didn't try to "coach" her husband, but her knowledge and interest in his life said clearly, "Because you're so important to me, your interests are important to me, too."

At the end of our conversation, my huge pro-football friend made a comment I've never forgotten: "Sometime I'll have to tell you how much my wife's taught me about refinishing antiques. I wouldn't be surprised if learning about one of her big interests is where I end up after football."

For this couple, being committed to each other meant showing interest in the things they individually valued. The message came over loud and clear that because of that attitude, they felt secure in each other's love and commitment. That security level showed clearly in their lives and the quality of love between them.

Security results when a man and a woman say to each other, "You're so valuable to me that no matter what happens in life, I'm going to commit myself to you. You're so valuable, I'm going to spend the rest of my life proving to you my pledge to love you."

Remains Tender During a Trial

One afternoon I was very late coming home from boating with my son Greg. I had taken the car, which left Norma with only our mini–motor home for transportation. She waited and waited, but when I was several hours later than I had predicted, she decided to take our mini–motor home to the grocery store.

Granted, our motor home is not the easiest thing to handle in the world. I'd already had my share of close calls when it came time to park or back the vehicle out. But Norma re-defined the term "close call" as she tried to back the camper out of the driveway.

She had almost made it out from under the carport when she turned the wheel the wrong way and sheared off an entire section of the roof. And if that wasn't bad enough, the falling roof bounced off the hood of the camper, scraping away paint and leaving a deep dent in its wake.

When I pulled into the driveway an hour later, I couldn't believe my eyes. Looking at the gaping hole in the roof, my first response was to look at the sky to see if the tornado was still around, but one look at our mobile home told me that it was Mother Norma, not Mother Nature, who had caused this catastrophe.

A love that lasts forever

communicates that someone is valuable

through actions of kindness.

I instantly wanted to order her out of the house and ask her questions like, "Where did you get your driver's license? From a gumball machine at Shop-mart?!"

Instead, I sat in my car, with my hands frozen on the steering wheel, praying, "Lord, You have to give me strength. Every fiber in my body wants to lecture my wife now and not be gentle with her. This is one of those pressure situations, and I know I have a choice. Lord, help me figure out what I'm going to do." Turning to my son Greg I asked him, 'What do you think I ought to do?'"

Greg said, "Dad, why don't you do what you teach?"

"That's a good idea," I said.

But all the while I was praying for the strength to be tender. Being tender at such a moment is definitely not natural. You have to take off the comfortable old nature of lectures and anger, and put on the new nature of tenderness (see Ephesians 4:22–24). This can be excruciatingly difficult.

Finally, I got out of the car and walked toward the piece of roof lying in the driveway, but just as I got up to the camper, Norma came flying around the side of the house.

I fought off the voice ringing in my mind, *Lecture her! Lecture her!* and I did what didn't feel "natural" at the time. I simply held her in my arms and gently patted her on the back. I hadn't spoken one word when finally, Norma pulled away and said, "Oh, look what I did! I wrecked the motor home and knocked off the roof." Then she added, "And I told the neighbors across the street what I did, and they're watching to see how you're going to respond."

Thankfully, I hadn't given the neighbors anything to gossip about by exploding at

A love that lasts forever offers tenderness at the moment of vulnerability during a crisis.

Norma. I just put my arms around her again and gently called her by my favorite affectionate name for her:

"Norm, listen. You know I love you. You're more important to me than campers and roofs. I know you didn't do this on purpose, and you're feeling really bad about it."

TENDERNESS TRANSFORMS TENSION

At that very moment, I could feel Norma relaxing. What's more, I immediately felt better myself as my own anger drained out of me and was replaced by feelings of tenderness. While it's hard to explain, I could tell that instead of being pulled apart, we were actually growing *stronger* as a result of the trial.

After a few more minutes of talking and holding her, Norma went on with whatever she was doing, and I went out to the garage to lay my hands on the few tools I had. After taking a deep breath, I said to Greg, "Well, I'd better get at it."

Just then, from out of nowhere, a friend from my church pulled into our driveway. This wasn't just any ordinary friend. He was a local contractor driving a pickup filled with hammers, saws, lumber, paint, and a long ladder. He jumped out and said, "Okay, Gary. Let's get at it!"

"Where did you come from?" I asked in disbelief.

Apparently our good neighbors across the street weren't only watching my reactions to Norma. They had also been calling everyone around town to talk about our hole in the roof. Ironically, my friend had been one of the first to hear the news. With his expert help, and without exaggeration, we had our impromptu skylight patched and repainted within two hours.

As I went to bed that night with Norma snuggled up to me, I was amazed that I had actually done something right for a change, during a stressful situation. What would I have normally done? I could have zapped the life right out of her emotionally with angry words and lectures, and it would have taken days for us to feel our way back to each other.

If I hadn't known about the power of gentleness, I'm sure I would have acted as I had in the past and blown up. This time I didn't, and amazingly, it made all the difference. The old Gary Smalley might have lost it. The new one followed a biblical blueprint for turning away anger, and it made even a stressful event a time of closeness.

I learned an important lesson that day; it's one I've seen repeated time and time again in my life and in the lives of others.

Simply put, that lesson is: *Remaining tender during a trial is one of the most powerful ways to build an intimate relationship* (James 1:19–20).

Most people's basic bent during times of stress is to lash out or lecture—or both—

especially if the predicament is somebody else's fault. But tenderness, above and beyond the call of our human nature, is a transformer, an energizer of those around us.

Since I wasn't fortunate enough to have a father who knew how to be tender to his wife, I wasn't aware that softness during stressful times was even an option until several years into my marriage. And that's when I learned that one of a person's greatest needs is to be comforted, especially during those moments in life when the roof falls in.

Ephesians 4:32 is your instruction booklet for becoming a tender-hearted person. In these verses are two powerful ways to be tender-hearted. The first is, "Be kind . . . to one another," then, "forgiving each other, just as in Christ God forgave you."

In other words, when it comes to being tender, kindness, gentleness, and forgiveness are like battery packs. They are what gives tenderness its punch. Combine a "kind" act with a tender touch, and the results can be life-changing.

TENDERNESS AND TIMING

Often the time to give someone a gentle word of encouragement or a meaningful touch is obvious. Sometimes, though, especially for people like me who do not come from a "high touch" background, it's hard to recognize the not-so-obvious times we need to be tender. What do we do then?

I'll never forget what one woman told me:

"If my husband would only put his arms around me when I'm feeling blue, and not give me a nonstop lecture or pep talk about 'counting it all joy,' it would transform our marriage."

"Have you ever *told* him what you need?" I asked.

"Are you kidding? He'd be embarrassed and so would I," she said with a laugh.

"This may come as a surprise to you," I said, "but he probably doesn't know how to be tender with you. He's been trained to lecture. Perhaps he needs some training in what genuine tenderness is."

"That makes sense to me," she said. "Many times when I'm crying and upset, he'll ask, 'What do you want me to do?' And I just flare up and say, *'If I have to tell you what to do, then that would ruin it!'*"

A husband should ask his wife, and a wife her husband, to define "tenderness" in their own terms. How should he hold her for her to feel safe and loved—when is the best time for her to be soft and sympathetic with him? A wife or husband shouldn't expect his or her mate to be a mind reader when it comes to meeting the very important needs in this area.

Most of us aren't good emotional mind readers anyway, and too few of us come from comforting backgrounds, so we don't know the nonverbal signals that say, "Please hold me." While attempting to talk about being tender may seem awkward at first, just being willing to talk about this much-needed skill tends to bring energy and life to a relationship.

Tenderness is catching when it's communicated in a home—whether it's a shared word, a gentle touch, or an act of forgiveness. It results in renewed energy between loved ones — and is another important way to build a loving, lasting relationship.

Learns How to Reach the Deepest Levels of Verbal Intimacy

I frequently ask couples to name one thing they believe could improve their marriage above everything else. Without exception, the answer has come through loud and clear: "We need better communication!"

Why such a high priority on communication? Because good communication is the key to what all of us who marry basically want . . . to love and be loved. We want to share our lives with someone who loves us unconditionally. We want to grow old with a mate who has valued us, understood us, and helped us feel safe in sharing our deepest feelings and needs. We want to make love last forever. And this type of loving relationship is most often attained by couples who have learned how to reach the deepest levels of verbal intimacy.

COMMUNICATING—BUT AT WHAT LEVEL?

Marriage researchers have helped us understand that there are five levels of intimacy in communication, moving from the superficial to the most meaningful. The more often a husband

A love that lasts forever is built on

communication that gets to the heart of

what both people feel and need.

and wife reach and remain on the fourth and fifth levels, the more satisfying their marriage.

When we communicate on the first level, we speak in clichés: "How did your day go?" "Fine." "Give me five!" "What's happening?" Think about it. Does conversation at this level mean much? A question like "How are you?" may be more than a cliché, especially in marriage, but it's often asked just as superficially in a domestic setting as it is by a store clerk you've never met before.

At the second level of communication, we share facts—just information. "Hey, it looks pretty wet today, doesn't it?" "Watch out for that new road construction." "Did you hear the latest about the president?" Like level one, this is pretty shallow communication, and it's still relatively safe. Not many major marital wars start this way.

At the third level, we state our opinions. Here is where communication feels a bit more unsafe and conflict may arise. "How can anyone vote for that person? He has no experience." If we feel insecure in our marriage, we tend to steer clear of this level. Though most couples do get to this level, most of our conversation, even with family, rarely goes beyond it to the deeper levels.

The fourth level is when we say what we're feeling. "I was really hurt by what my father said on the phone last night." Opening up this way can be scary, but we can reach the deeper levels of loving and being loved only when we put ourselves at risk of having our feelings

A love that lasts forever takes the risk to ask,

"What are you feeling right now?"

misunderstood or ridiculed. In fact, one of the healthiest questions we can ask is, "What are you feeling right now?"

The fifth level is where we reveal our needs. "I just need for you to hold me for a few minutes," you might say after hearing about the serious illness of a good friend. To risk at this level of verbal intimacy, we have to feel secure in the relationship. Let's see how a couple with a strong marriage and good communication skills might work their way quickly to this level.

Suppose, for instance, that a conversation starts at the third level with the husband saying to his wife, "Hey, you're drenched! Why don't you ever remember to put your umbrella in the car?" That's an opinion that his wife should keep an umbrella handy.

She responds at the fourth level by saying, "Do you know how I feel today? I feel like somebody ran over my foot at work. It's been a tough day! And with that cute comment, you're now standing on my foot!"

Instantly he knows how his spouse feels. He can now encourage her to move to the fifth level by asking, "What do you need tonight? What would it take to make you feel as if your foot is being massaged and soothed? What can I do?"

She might respond by saying, "You know that movie we were planning to go see? I don't really feel like going tonight. I'm beat! I would love a hug, and I just want to talk and be with you. But first, I would like to be alone for a while, to relax and kind of cool down."

Those are needs, and expressing them is the deepest level of verbal intimacy.

The understanding husband might say, "Okay, let's do that. I wanted to go to that movie, but we don't have to go tonight. We can go tomorrow. What do you think?" That's a mutually satisfying relationship, where both people's needs are expressed and they have the flexibility of give-and-take.

Our goal as a married couple should be to go into those fourth and fifth more satisfying levels of communication more easily and frequently. But again, the key to deep verbal intimacy is feeling safe to share our feelings and needs and sensing that our feelings and needs are valued by our mate. Having the self-control to listen lovingly without overreacting or misunderstanding keeps the lines open. The caution I would interject here is that we need to speak in love, measure our words carefully, and only make requests that we can reasonably expect our mate to respond to favorably.

Allows Conflict to Become a Doorway to Intimacy

ost of us dislike and try to avoid conflicts, especially with our spouses. For peace lovers, this chapter has both bad news and good. The bad news is that we're always going to have conflicts. Our valued individuality—including our personality and gender differences—makes them inevitable. But the good news is that not only can we reduce our conflicts, we can also use them to move into deeper intimacy in any relationship.

To illustrate how conflicts can lead to deeper intimacy, let me relate (with their permission) a story about our daughter, Kari, and her husband, Roger. It is very typical of young married couples. Roger heard that his mom and dad were coming to visit. He was pretty excited about that visit, because he loves to eat. He especially loves a big breakfast, and his mom used to cook him one every day. She's that kind of loving mother, and he was the baby of the family. I know how that goes, since I was the baby of my family. But then I got married and found out that wives don't always wait on you the way your mother did. Well, Roger has

A love that lasts forever looks beyond

disagreement and conflict to identify

what needs are begging to be met.

learned the same lesson. And also like me, he sometimes says things that have the opposite effect of what he intended.

So, thinking as a male can, when he heard his folks were coming, Roger said, "Finally, I can have one of those big breakfasts again!" He will admit that this comment was in praise of his mother but that it also was meant as an editorial comment about Kari's not cooking him breakfasts. Maybe she'd take the hint. That made sense to him, but it didn't sit well with Kari. Instantly—wham!—conflict. Kari went silent.

Fortunately Roger is a sensitive and loving husband. He doesn't want to offend Kari. He wants to make sure everything is going great. This happened before their first child, our grandson Michael Thomas, was born, and already Roger was concerned about providing a healthy family atmosphere. So he opened the door offered by that conflict and asked, "Kari, how did my comment make you feel?"

Now, word pictures are great for expressing feelings. Roger and Kari have developed their own word-picture method that conveys instantly how they're feeling. Their method uses fruit imagery, and it goes like this: If something happens but it's not a big deal, she'll say, "You just hit me with a raisin." If it's a little bigger deal, she'll say he hit her with an orange. If it's bigger still, she'll say it was a cantaloupe. But this time she said, "You just hit me with a twenty-five-pound watermelon—wham!—and drove me right into the ground." And he instantly entered into her feelings.

Seeing his desire to work things out, she went on to explain that his comment had made her feel inadequate, not as good as his mom. She thought, *What about all the great dinners*

I make? How come he isn't saying, "Wow, your dinners are just wonderful! Your dinners blow my mom's dinners away"?

Roger had a different view. He wasn't saying he had a problem with her dinners. He was saying, "I'm not getting breakfast."

Back to Kari's perspective: It's pretty hard to make a big breakfast when you're a teacher and getting up at six (before he gets up) just to be ready for work on time. And what he said was not the way to motivate her to want to make his breakfast. (I think she had even mentioned to him before they married, "I don't do breakfast," but I guess that's the kind of thing you overlook at the time you're just starting to grow in love.)

What came out of this conflict? He knew how she felt, he reinforced how much he loved her, and he found out one important way to avoid conflict in the future.

That's an example of using conflict as a doorway to intimacy, of getting past opinions to feelings. When conflict is used this way, we don't need to be afraid of it; it actually becomes a good thing that moves the relationship forward.

We actually need to have disagreements. That doesn't mean we go looking for fights. Should we keep fighting just so we can enjoy the deeper intimacy of making up? By no means.

But when conflicts do occur, they can bring benefits (produce pearls) if we use them in the right way. With that hope in mind, let's take a closer look at the anatomy of conflict, beginning with why it happens in the first place.

The Underlying Reasons for Conflict

Conflicts—disagreements that can escalate into fights—occur for a number of reasons.

Power and Control

Who is going to make the decisions? Who's the boss? When there is vying for authority— boom! Conflict. It happens when we least expect it.

Insecurity

If you think your mate is drifting and creating distance, for instance, you're likely to feel insecure, and conflict is a natural result.

Some personalities hold things in for a long time, and then they explode. It might be because they don't feel safe to bring up those things when they first are perceived as a problem. In time the unresolved anger explodes "out of the blue."

Differences in Values

He thinks it's okay to drink alcohol at every meal, and she can't stand it. She thinks it's fine to tell people someone's not home when a call comes in, and he thinks that's lying. He wants to attend church every Sunday, and she likes to go only at Christmas and Easter.

It's important to remember here that not all differences can be eliminated. In such cases, it's healthy to say to each other, "We'll never agree on this issue, but I still love you, and I hope we can learn more about each other's feelings and needs through this conflict."

A love that lasts forever sees conflict as

a doorway to greater intimacy and knowledge.

Competition

Some people can't stand to lose at anything, even a casual game of checkers. Or perhaps the husband is bothered by the fact that his wife earns more than he does, and he's determined to outdo her in that area.

Personal Differences

Couples fight over normal male-female differences and normal personality differences. We can count on those two areas to bring a continual flow of conflicts.

Misunderstood Feelings and Unmet Needs

I believe this is the major reason for conflict—when one or, more likely, both spouses have unmet needs. Dr. Stephen Covey says this in a different way. He claims that all conflicts are caused by unfulfilled expectations in "roles and goals." For example, one spouse may think, *That's not what you're supposed to do in our relationship. I fix the car, and you fix the meals.* Or one may say to the other, "I've always wanted to go on in my education. You knew that. We'll just have to go without that new couch until I finish." We expect others to know our needs and feelings, in fact, even if we haven't mentioned them.

It's been extremely helpful to me to understand that whenever I'm in conflict with someone, one of two things is occurring: Someone's feelings aren't being valued and understood, or someone's needs are not being valued and met. Needs unnecessarily go unmet when we get too busy—when the spouse and kids aren't getting enough time with us or there's just not enough conversation.

What *Doesn't* Work in Conflict

For a marriage to grow as a result of conflict—for healing to occur after conflict—we need to learn to move toward resolution. But some patterns just don't do the job as well as we'd like.

What doesn't work for healing resolution? For starters, withdrawing into yourself. I used to do this because it's what I often saw my father doing. If you withdraw, however, you don't get your needs met, your spouse's needs don't get met, and your relationship suffers. So withdrawing is not the solution. In fact, Dr. Scott Stanley says that the worst thing for a marriage is when the husband clams up and distances himself from the family.

Yielding—giving in—isn't a satisfactory pattern, either. While one person wins and therefore peace prevails for a season, the other person loses, and ultimately, the relationship also loses. If both partners don't win, the relationship is weakened.

A third pattern? You could be the winner—the opposite of yielding. But again, one of you ends up a loser, so the relationship loses.

How about compromise? Isn't that healthy? Sometimes you just don't have time to

resolve the issue right then, so you each settle for half a loaf. But remember that compromise is only a temporary solution because it's still a win-lose situation for both of you and for your relationship. Postponing is okay, but if you don't get back to the dispute, you lose a doorway to a deeper intimacy.

EVERYBODY WINS

Let's work through another pattern in which everybody wins—both parties and the relationship. Here you keep working on the conflict until you both feel good about the solution. The issue is resolved. You both know your feelings are being understood. And you both feel your needs are being met. It may take some deep conversation over a couple of days or longer, but your attitude and approach are always saying, Let's work to resolve this issue, where we both feel like winners.

It's not always possible to come to a resolution where you both feel good about the outcome. But it is possible to restate your commitment to each other at any point. You can say things like, "I still love you and always will. We can't seem to agree on this issue, but I'm committed to you for life, and I'll never stop loving you over any disagreement." Such commitment and lasting love have a way of softening the dispute.

PERSONAL KEYS TO INTIMACY

Conflict is a doorway into intimacy because it's a way to discover who a person is. As soon as we hit the wall and are in conflict, we have to open a door so we can walk through it to find out what the other person feels and needs. Instead of reverting to silence or clichés, we can adopt an attitude that says, I'm kind of glad we're having this conflict because it'll result in both of us knowing more about each other and loving each other more.

Norma and I were recently locked in a prolonged argument about my travel schedule. I still speak a great deal across the country, and we don't live near a major airport. So I wanted to investigate the possibility of leasing a company plane to use on speaking trips. But Norma has been against the idea of small planes for quite some time.

As we went back and forth on this issue, it was increasingly clear that we weren't going to agree. So we stepped back to ask, "What are our deepest feelings about renting a plane?"

I found out that she fears the smaller planes because of all the publicity that comes when one crashes. She feels they're unsafe, so she believes riding in them is taking an unnecessary risk. I also learned that she wants me to value her uneasiness about the plane and to respect her expression of her true feelings.

Remember the breakfast story from the beginning of this chapter? After Roger asked Kari how she felt and she told him, he then asked what she needed. "What can I do to show you I love you?" She replied, "I need for you to praise me for the things I do and the things I get excited about doing." In other words, she needed him to do more than just avoid insulting her; she needed to hear words of appreciation for the things she does. And since then, he has made an effort to give her that praise. He's become the kind of husband dads hope their daughters will find. (My special thanks to the Gibsons, his parents.)

OPPORTUNITIES TO EXPRESS AFFECTION

Conflicts can open a doorway to intimacy by surfacing feelings and needs. But conflicts also provide an opportunity to express physical and emotional affection. We all need to be hugged. We all need to be loved on.

Conflicts are inevitable in any relationship. But the good news overrides the bad: I challenge you to see any disagreements with your spouse as a doorway to intimacy. Let conflicts be that doorway into a better understanding of how you both feel and what you each need. Open the door. Walk through—and you will learn more about the delights of marriage than you ever dreamed possible.

If a conflict is ultimately going to draw a couple closer together, they need a set of "fighting rules." That list becomes the key to what I call the doorway to intimacy. If you don't have such boundaries on how you fight, you may say or do any number of things that shut down communication—that slam the door on intimacy.

THE SMALLEY "FIGHTING RULES"

1. First clarify what the actual conflict is. Make sure that you understand your partner as clearly as you can before proceeding to a resolution. Listening is vital here! Endeavor to work for understanding in two key areas: your mate's feelings, and then, needs.

2. Stick to the issue at hand. Don't dredge up past hurts or problems, whether real or perceived. But if you tend to veer off the issue, you might want to see if there is any other key factor in this conflict, such as fatigue, low estrogen levels, low blood sugar, stress, work problems, or spiritual or emotional issues.

3. Maintain as much tender physical contact as possible. Hold hands.

4. Avoid sarcasm.

5. Avoid "you" statements. Use the words "I feel" or "I think." No past or future predictions ("You always . . ." "You won't ever . . .").

6. Don't use "hysterical" statements or exaggerations. ("This will never work out." "You're just like your father.")

7. Resolve any hurt feelings before continuing the conflict discussion. ("I shouldn't have said that. Will you forgive me?")

8. Don't resort to name-calling. Don't allow the conflict to escalate your tempers. If this happens, agree to continue the discussion later.

9. Avoid power statements and actions. For example: "I quit!" "You sleep on the couch tonight!" "You're killing me!" "I hate you!"

10. Don't use the silent treatment.

11. Keep your arguments as private as possible to avoid embarrassment.

12. Use the "drive-through" method of communication when arguing. (Repeat back what you think the other person is saying.)

13. Resolve your conflicts with win-win solutions; both parties agree with the solution or outcome of the argument. Work on resolution only after both understand feelings and needs.

14. Above all, strive to reflect honor in all your words and actions during the resolution of your conflicts.

Keeps Courtship Alive Long After the Wedding Day

uring courtship, romance is something that seems to overflow naturally. Let the years of marriage pass, however, and often romance slows to a thin trickle. Yet romance is an essential ingredient of a strong relationship.

Romance finds its place in a marriage right between the chapters that illustrate love as a decision of our will, and the sexual relationship, which involves our feelings and emotions. In many ways, romance is the bridge between the two. It's an important way we express honor to our spouse, and it provides the basis for a meaningful sex life.

Poetically, we could say that romance is the flame that glows on the candle of unconditional love; it's the act of honor that soothes and refreshes a marriage like a gentle spring rain; it's the fertile soil in which passion grows. But for those of us who didn't major in poetry, what is it in plain English?

Romance is the act of keeping your courtship alive long after the wedding day. Put another way, romance is an intimate friendship, celebrated with expressions of love reserved only for each other.

A love that lasts forever uses surprise,

spontaneity, and creativity in romance

to celebrate special moments.

Romance is a *relationship,* not an event. It's not something we do occasionally to stoke the fires of passion. Rather, it should be an ongoing, foundational part of our relationship, something that doesn't come and go like the tide, but flows as steadily as a river. An inescapable aspect of romance is being "best friends" with your spouse.

A key to blending friendship with romance is to take the time to explore each other's interests and then share them together. I recently saw a cartoon that captures this idea. The scene shows a couple walking happily hand in hand, looking deeply into each other's eyes, and obviously enjoying a conversation together. The caption read, "Romance happens when . . . he asks about her potted plants and she asks about the football scores." As unromantic as "sunflowers" and "screen passes" may seem, that cartoon really captures the essence of one important element of romance.

If you're not growing a friendship based on each other's shared interests—I can almost guarantee you that the romantic soil in your relationship is lacking the essential nutrients it needs.

WHAT'S YOUR ROMANTIC "TEN"?

Contrary to popular opinion, close romantic times don't just happen. With our overcommitted lifestyles, if we don't set our schedules, someone or something else will set them for us. Planning is the key. I know, you may be thinking, *But Gary! . . . Planning takes all the thrill out of it. Romance is supposed to be spontaneous!* No doubt spontaneity has its place; but it is crucial that we rid ourselves of the false notion that the secret to building a romantic relationship is the five o'clock phone call for a candlelight dinner at six.

By planning, what I mean is using the "twenty questions" method with your spouse. Husbands and wives should begin blending their recipe for romance together with:

"Honey, on a scale of one to ten, what's a romantic ten to you?"

It's a good idea to have paper and pen ready, to jot down each idea that is suggested. Next, "milk" these answers for added information. By "milking" I mean try to find out as much information as possible about what your spouse has told you by asking more questions about the idea.

For instance, if your spouse says, "I think it would be a ten to go on a skiing vacation," then you could ask, "Where would you want to go? What time of the year? What kind of snow would you like best? Would you need new ski clothes? What colors and styles? Where would we eat? Where would you like to stay? Would we meet friends there or go by ourselves? Would we do anything else besides ski?" The list could go on and on.

Each question you ask makes you a more insightful romantic. The more you know about what would be a "ten" for your spouse, the more you'll be able to understand his or her interests, and become more fully involved in them.

Why not sit down with your spouse and look at the year ahead? Find out each other's romantic tens, and schedule what you can into the calendar. It's amazing what anticipation does to heighten romance! Be sure to commit to making these dates a priority. If you don't, other things or other people will crowd them out of your schedule.

Developing a deep level of friendship through shared interests is the first essential ingredient in a romantic relationship. Discovering each other's relational "tens" and making plans to make them happen can also make a huge difference in the quality of our romantic times together. There's a third way to keep the courtship alive with our spouse.

CELEBRATE SPECIAL MOMENTS IN YOUR LIFE

Those who are wise romantics will realize that some special date or event every year can be used to fan the romantic flame. I recall one man who put together a very special celebration for his wife to honor her for a sacrifice she had made for him.

It was the eve of his graduation from a long, grueling master's degree program. Four years of intensive, full-time study had finally found him about to receive his diploma.

His wife planned a special party to which many of their friends were to come and help him celebrate the long-awaited "day of deliverance." Her husband, though, had other ideas. He secretly contacted each person who had received an invitation and told them he wanted to make the party a surprise in honor of *her*. Yes, there would be banners, streamers, and all the rest, but they would bear her name, not his.

He wanted to do something special to let her know how much he appreciated the years of sacrifice she'd devoted to his graduation.

A love that lasts forever finds romance in developing a friendship centered on shared interests.

Working full-time to put him through, and putting off her dreams of a house and family, had, in many ways, been harder on her than the long hours of study had been on him.

That night, when she realized what was going on, she could barely hold back the tears. Her husband asked a few people to share what they most appreciated about her. Then he stood before them, and with tender words of love and appreciation, expressed his gratitude for all she'd done for him. When he was through, they saluted her with an iced-tea toast.

It was a celebration of an experience they both shared, and by commemorating it in a special way, this husband created a lifelong, romantic memorial to his wife's love and dedication.

Birthdays, anniversaries, or holidays can become more than simply a traditional observance. They can be a personal opportunity to let your loved one know they are very special to you—in ways they'll never forget.

PUTTING ROMANCE IN THE DEEP FREEZE

Imagine the following scene. A man and woman are casually strolling arm in arm along a beautiful white sand beach. The waves gently wash ashore, and the sea gulls dart back and forth overhead. A full moon glimmers in the night sky, and the sand seems like an endless strand of silver dust. It's a romantic ending to a perfect day, until . . .

If you look more closely, you will see the look on her face. It isn't one of peace and love. It's one of frustration and anger. Why? The setting is all right, but something he did is all wrong.

Ten minutes before, she told him she wanted to take a quiet walk on the beach and talk. He agreed to the walk, which excited her—but he destroyed the romantic setting when he held her hand in one hand, and his fishing pole in the other.

"Hey, I've been casting for years," he told her. "I can talk and fish at the same time, no problem!"

This man broke the cardinal rules of romance:

1. *Make sure the romantic activity you're involved in receives your full, undivided attention.*

2. *Make sure you're doing the activity for your spouse's best interests, not yours.*

Any time I send Norma flowers, or give her a card, or do something special, I'm saying, "I love you." At the moment it is unclouded by hidden motives, but I can quickly ruin it for her. All I have to do is ask a favor or tell her about my plans for fishing with the guys that weekend, or intimate that what I've done "deserves" a romantic response, and it's as if I walked into the house saying, "Gee, honey . . . you're sure looking bad today."

The key to being romantic, then, is to concentrate on being *relational!* When that happens, and your spouse truly senses you desire a deep, intimate friendship, then the stage is set to enjoy the wonderful pleasures of physical intimacy.

Discovers the Secret to Sexual Satisfaction

Nothing in marriage is more misunderstood than the sexual union. It's more than the physical act that sexually unites a couple. There are actually four areas of the sexual relationship that need to be developed in concert with one another if a couple is to achieve maximum satisfaction. Before we look at these four areas, however, we have to recognize that men and women tend to see sex very differently.

MALE-FEMALE DIFFERENCES

In an ongoing study I've conducted with hundreds of couples over the years, I ask men and women privately and in groups how they would feel if they knew they would never again have sex with their mates. Almost all the women say, "It's really no big deal if I never have sex again with my husband." But they add quickly that it would be a big deal if they were never touched or kissed or romanced again.

When I ask men the same question, they're almost always incredulous. "Give up sex?"

A love that lasts forever

freely expresses feelings in mutual,

nonthreatened self-disclosure.

they say. "No way!" To ask a man to give up sex is to ask him to give up eating.

Why this huge difference between the views of men and women? It's not easy for some women to understand what testosterone does to a man. The hormone fires up a man sexually. (I know the image of the male driven by testosterone is a stereotype, but in this case it's an accurate one.)

To give wives a better idea, imagine you've just been informed by mail that you've won the grand prize in a national contest. You and your husband will be whisked off to a tropical island for ten days of first-class service at a four-star resort. You'll also be given fifteen hundred dollars a day in spending money, unlimited luxury limousine service—in other words, the works! Naturally, you can't wait for your husband to walk in the door so you can tell him the good news.

Now imagine that when he does come home, you greet him by saying you have some wonderful news. But he responds, "Not now, dear. I'm really tired, so I think I'm going to take a nap." As he walks to the bedroom, he adds, "Don't tell anyone else the news. I want to be the first to hear it."

When I ask women how they would feel in this situation, most say they would be highly frustrated.

A man's testosterone level makes him feel as if he has won the grand prize . . . almost every day! He can't wait to "tell" you about it. But a disinterested wife responds, "Let's talk about it tomorrow." Imagine the way that makes him feel. Some husbands are so highly testosterone-loaded that they're literally trembling on the other side of the bed while you're drifting off to sleep. Perhaps that will help you understand why he gets frustrated when you put off his physical advances.

FOUR VITAL AREAS OF SEXUAL SATISFACTION

Sex is more than a physical act. Good sex is the reflection of a good relationship. It's the icing on top of what's right in a marriage. I've learned that fulfilling sex has at least four separate aspects that work together—they must work together:

Intercourse literally means "to get to know someone intimately." In our culture, we have reduced the word to refer only to the act of sex. Conversely, we've nearly forgotten a traditional meaning of the verb "to know"—which was "to have sexual intercourse." Biblical history starts the whole human lineage with this line: "And Adam knew Eve his wife; and she conceived . . ." (Genesis 4:1, KJV). The two words *intercourse* and *knowledge* are closely aligned.

Verbal Intercourse

In earlier times, people used the word *intercourse* when speaking of an intimate conversation. Obviously, we have to be sensitive to our current culture, so it's not advisable to have a discussion with your next-door neighbor and then yell over the fence, "It sure was good having intercourse with you earlier today!"

But verbal intercourse is vital to a healthy sex life. It involves getting to know your mate through conversation and spending time together. This is especially significant to most

A love that lasts forever makes—even schedules—
time for talk. "Tell me about your world.
I'll tell you about mine."

women, who are amazed that men can have sex at almost any time without regard to the quality of the relationship. The women usually want to connect with their partners through verbal intimacy before they can enjoy the physical act. As a couple, work at giving each other the time you need to relax, talk, and listen to each other.

Emotional Intercourse

Sharing deep feelings with each other is emotional intercourse, and it's vital to sexual satisfaction. It's that sense of connectedness that occurs when you're both tracking on the same emotional level. This involves conversations that deal with more than facts alone. Any conversation might start with facts. Then any fact in a relationship can be connected to emotions with the question: "How does that set of facts make you feel?" This is especially significant to women. They are often most responsive to sexual intercourse when the entire relationship is open and loving—when they feel that their husband understands and values their feelings.

Dave and Vicki were struggling with this when Dave first came to see me. "I'll shoot straight with you, Gary," he said. "I'm not getting any sex from my wife, and I'm very frustrated."

As I listened to him explain his situation, I suggested he go back to his wife and seek to communicate his feelings through the use of an emotional word picture. "The analogy will get out on the table the deep feelings you have about this issue," I told him.

So that's exactly what he did. And then she responded with a powerful word picture of her own.

"Honey, we have a problem," he told her that night. "I want you to hear how I describe it."

"All right," Vicki agreed.

"When I'm away from you at work, I feel like I'm out in the middle of the desert. It's steaming hot, and I'm slowly baking. But when I get home, I feel like I've entered an oasis."

Vicki smiled and said, "Well, that's good."

"Not really," Dave went on. "You see, when I come home, you look so good to me that I want to enjoy our relationship completely."

"Meaning what?" she asked.

"Sex," Dave answered. "We just don't have sex anymore, so I feel that instead of being in an oasis, part of the oasis is a mirage. The beauty of the oasis doesn't all seem to exist."

He sat there for a moment in silence. As tenderly as he could, he asked her, "How can I make the mirage back into the real oasis we once had?"

Vicki had been listening, and they were connecting on an emotional level. After a minute she responded, "I'll tell you how to return to the oasis. I'll even do for you what you just did for me. I'll paint an emotional word picture to make it clear.

"I feel as if I'm one of your prized rare antique books from the nineteenth century," she began. "Early in our marriage, you would pick me up and admire me, make sure I was free from dust, polish the gold-leaf edges, and just take good care of me overall."

Dave smiled at her knowingly.

"But something has happened to that rare book," she continued. "You don't care for it the way you used to. It has become dusty sitting on the shelf. The gold leaf is covered with a tarnish that could be removed if it just had a little attention. Now I'm just one of many rare books."

She was getting through to him for the first time in a long while, because he responded, "How can I give this book more of the attention it deserves?"

Vicki was able to tell him what was important to her—things like saying "I love you," and even things that Dave considered unrelated, like spending time with the kids. She also remembered fondly the days when Dave used to send her flowers and cards.

The more the two of them talked on a deep emotional level, the more they were able to help each other. This communication at the deep levels of feelings and needs changed Dave and Vicki's sexual relationship into a richer, fuller, and mutually satisfying one. It's still not perfect, but then I've never met a couple for which it was.

Physical Intercourse

Now we get to the real thing, right? Slow down. What we tend to zero in on is actually a small part of the physical relationship. When thinking of physical intercourse, think more in terms of touching, caressing, hugging, kissing, and romancing.

From my interviews and counseling with women, I've concluded that most women need eight to twelve meaningful touches a day to keep their energy level high and experience a sense of connectedness with their mate—a hug, a squeeze of the hand, a pat on the shoulder, a gentle kiss. There are approximately five million touch receptors in the human body—more than two million in the hands alone. The right kind of touch releases a pleasing and healing flow of chemicals in the bodies of both the toucher and the touched. The whole relationship will be much better if we give each other a lot of tender physical touch throughout the day.

Spiritual Intercourse

Spiritual intercourse may be the highest level of intimacy. A husband and wife can know each other as they both turn to and know God—heart to heart. Scripture writers repeatedly used a marriage metaphor to refer to the relationship God wants to have with those who turn to Him. And the Spirit of God has an otherworldly ability to draw two people into harmony, being "one" in spirit.

A man and wife can grow spiritually intimate as they pray together, worship God together, attend study groups or retreats together, or simply discuss spiritual lessons and insights. Spiritual intercourse involves knowing one another in the context of a shared faith. And through that faith a couple sees the value and meaning of things that would otherwise be meaningless.

The blending of these four aspects of intercourse provides the complete context for a healthier sexual relationship. They're like the four sides of a building . . . all are essential for a sound and lasting structure.

IMPROVING SEXUAL INTIMACY

Once you're establishing the verbal, emotional, physical, and spiritual connections, you can follow some additional steps to improve the sexual dimension of your marriage. First I'll give five general suggestions that either a wife or a husband can try to enhance the physical act of sex. Then I'll offer some suggestions that are specific to each of the partners.

Both Partners

Take the initiative sexually. This is generally appreciated by your partner, especially if it's not your usual mode of operation. The change of pace will energize your experience.

Take care with your appearance. Your spouse will value the effort you make to look attractive.

Take more time to enjoy the sexual experience. Routinized sex—relegated to ten minutes after the TV late news on Saturday night—is the kiss of death to a vibrant sex life. Don't be in a hurry. Think in terms of the four areas of intercourse we've discussed, and then take an unhurried walk through all of them. It can make a sexual evening very special.

Pay attention to the atmosphere in which you'll make love. Beyond candlelight, soft music, and a fire's glow (which are all great ideas), don't overlook some basics like a locked door. Visitors aren't welcome, even if they're members of the family. This is a time for husband and wife, and no unpleasant surprises are appreciated.

Express your desire. Many couples feel that the sexual act expresses how much they are attracted to each other, and they use sex in place of verbalizing the desire to be together. But words such as "I love you," "I need you," "I'm crazy about you," "You look great," and "I'd marry you all over again" have an encouraging and stimulating power all their own. So tell your mate often how much you enjoy being with him or her.

For Men

What would your wife say if she were asked how you could improve your sex life? My research shows that women often answer along these lines:

Be romantic. Women love to feel connection with their spouses, and nothing accomplishes this better than romance. By becoming a student of your wife, you can learn the best way to produce romantic feelings within her. For some, it is flowers, cards, or a small gift. For others, it's sharing in work around the house and lightening her load. Still others look to a night out on the town, a concert, or dinner in a nice restaurant.

Men can be a little rougher than their spouses in sex. But women love tenderness in a man. They always have, too—this

A love that lasts forever is renewed

and energized by tender touch.

is not just some "sensitive nineties man" fad. Women respond to romance, and most desire more of it.

Take time with foreplay. You cannot lose by spending extra time touching, hugging, and cuddling your wife. These acts are like giving her an injection of pure energy. Ask your wife where and how she likes to be touched, and be responsive to her needs. Conversely, if something you desire makes her uncomfortable, respect her wishes.

Remember also to freely touch your wife with caresses that won't necessarily lead to sex. Praise her, tell her how desirable she is, and give her spontaneous hugs.

Make yourself sexy. Stan is a typical guy. He loves his wife, Andrea, and is always ready to make love at a moment's notice. Andrea is consistently amazed by this attribute. She was recently surprised when he came in the back door after gardening in the muddy dirt for four hours. Sweaty, dirty, smelly, and unkempt as he was, when he saw her bending over in the kitchen, he let out a low wolf whistle and offered her an invitation for some immediate fun.

Andrea, like most women, finds her husband attractive, but that isn't always enough. Did he really expect her to be interested in a sexual encounter after he had just spent four hours in the mud? No way!

At first Stan was hurt by her cool response. He prided himself on keeping in shape and looking good. So Andrea had to explain that she wasn't rejecting him. She just felt more inclined toward making love if there was a "total package," as she put it. That included a clean and scrubbed, freshly shaven ("I hate stubble," she says), cologne-wearing Stan; clean sheets on the bed; soft light; and a classical CD playing softly in the background.

Andrea's reaction had nothing to do with Stan's fear that he was overweight or soft in areas that were once muscular. It was more about atmosphere. Stan needed to listen carefully so he could learn how to provide her idea of the perfect evening. It's only fair that he learn from her because, another time, he'll want her to try his idea of romance (in some room other than the bedroom when the kids are away at their grandparents' house).

For Women

Many wives wish they could find the key to unlock the sexual aspect of their husband's life. So here are some ideas specifically for women.

Understand his tremendous sexual needs. As discussed earlier, the two of you probably view sex from different perspectives. More than likely, he desires sex more often than you.

With that insight, there may be occasions when you're willing to have sex even if all four areas of intimacy are not in place for you. This should only be once in a while, however, not a regular pattern. He needs to be sensitive to your needs just as you're sensitive to his. For example, if your hormones make you wish your husband were in Siberia for several days a month, he needs to understand that and be patient.

Find out what he really enjoys. A man is thrilled when his wife asks him what he likes in regard to sex and then gives it a try. This does not mean you have to violate your inner convictions or participate in a sexual activity you find offensive. But there may be many things your husband thinks of in his fantasy life that you could fulfill for him and enjoy yourself.

The sexual relationship is a place where creativity should shine. Sex was never meant to be dull, boring, or routine. Take the initiative to instigate some variety in your sex life. Few men will respond, "No, this isn't what I want. Let's go back to doing it exactly the same as we have for the last twenty years."

Make yourself sexy. Having read my account of Stan and Andrea, a woman could conclude that nothing is necessary on her part to keep the sexual fires alive. But the reality is that a balance needs to be achieved. Just as a woman appreciates the "total package" from her husband, so a man is entitled to the same consideration from his wife.

You'll want to have those magical occasions when you take a leisurely bath, slide into something sexy, spray a little perfume around, dim the lights, and turn on the station that plays the late-night love songs. Your husband will enjoy that atmosphere just as you do. It's another way to contribute to the variety that's so helpful to a healthy sexual relationship.

Don't settle for anything but the best. Don't let your sexual relationship deteriorate into just the physical act. Enrich your life together in all four areas of intimacy and watch your sexual love relationship become a love that lasts forever.

1.   You're both home from work at the end of the day. Set aside a fifteen-minute period at some point to discuss—reflect on—your respective day's activities.

2.   Make a rule that the TV is off during dinner, encouraging conversation. For that hour, let the answering machine take all phone calls except emergencies.

3.   Write a monthly date night into your schedule that cannot be broken.

4.   If your schedule permits, get together for lunch once a week—even if you're just brown-bagging it in the park.

5.   As a couple, attend one of your children's sports games or other performances. It's amazing how conversation can develop while you sit and watch your child or on the way to and from the game.

6.   Take a walk together after dinner. It's a good time to talk, and it's also good for you physically.

7.   If you are allowed some flexibility in your work schedule, go in late one day—after the kids have all gone off to school. Enjoy the hour with your spouse.

8.   Read a magazine article or book together that you both feel will stimulate a discussion.

9. Don't be afraid to use baby-sitters just to give you time alone to talk.

10. Write each other little notes that begin, "I have something amazing to talk with you about the next time we're together."

11. Once or twice a year, plan a weekend getaway for just the two of you.

12. Ask your best friend to hold you accountable to meet with your mate at least once a week for a meaningful conversation.

Practices Responsible Marriage Banking

I had my own unique financial system when Norma and I were first married: I wrote checks as long as I had them in my book—until I ran out of checks; I hoped—or assumed—there was enough in the bank to cover them.

But often, Norma would confront me: "We're overdrawn again."

"We can't be," I'd answer with a grin. "I still have checks in my book. It's impossible."

Sometimes she would be in tears. "I can't keep track of this. It's driving me crazy."

We also disagreed about when to pay bills. Norma preferred to pay them as soon as they came. But I wanted to hold on to our money as long as possible, paying our bills at the end of the month, just before payday. I liked the idea of having money, because you never know when an emergency might come up. With my check-writing habits, however, there wasn't always enough left at the end of the month to pay all the bills, let alone to save for emergencies.

"We have two late notices on this one bill," Norma would say, exasperated.

"Don't worry about it," I'd respond, which was not what she wanted to hear. My philosophy

A love that lasts forever

"deposits" more than it "withdraws."

was that you don't have to do anything until you get the fourth or fifth notice. You just keep shuffling late notices to the bottom of the pile until they appear at the top again and can't be ignored any longer.

Then the day came when Norma had taken all she could. She tearfully approached me once more and laid all the bills, her checkbook, and the budget in my lap. "I've had it!" she declared. "I can't take it anymore. From now on, this area is all yours. It's up to you whether we sink or swim." Years later, she admitted her despair that day: She figured she was really giving away our home, our car, and the rest of our financial life, because there was no way I would be able to handle it properly.

Fortunately, with the pressure on, I decided to learn how to be responsible. I got some help, grew to respect a budget, and worked my way out of the mess I had created. For the next fifteen years, I kept the books and paid the bills. And as I started to do all this, I learned a crucial but simple principle: You've got to have more money in the bank than you spend every month. Income has to exceed outgo. That's about as basic as family finance gets.

The principle is the same for a marriage that will stand the test of time: Make sure you are making more "deposits" to your spouse than "withdrawals."

Basics of Marital Banking

Before we discuss what I call marital banking, we need to define a few terms.

A "deposit" is anything positive, security-producing—anything that gives your mate energy. It's a gentle touch, a listening ear, a verbalized "I love you," a fun, shared experience; the list could go on and on. Temperament, gender, and birth order influence one's personal definition of a deposit. Going for long walks in the woods with a spouse may energize an introvert in the same way a houseful of holiday company (entertaining) energizes an extrovert.

A "withdrawal" is anything sad or negative—anything that drains energy from your mate. It's a harsh word, an unkept promise, being ignored, being hurt, being controlled; the list could be long. Some withdrawals differ from temperament to temperament; something perceived as a withdrawal for one person might be a deposit for another person. But too much control or being absent too much, physically or emotionally, is always a major withdrawal.

The more you keep a positive balance in your relationship account, with "giving" deposits exceeding "draining" withdrawals, the more secure that relationship will be. There's something very basic about the saying "If you're happy, I'm happy." If you're energized, I'm energized. Enthusiasm—for life, for romance, for "us"—is contagious.

And if your marriage is in rough shape because you've been making a lot more withdrawals than deposits, beginning now with a concerted effort to make deposits can help you turn things around faster than anything else I've seen.

Now let's look in more detail at how this principle works.

Your Personal Banking History

You and your spouse both have a personal-relationship banking history. As in real banking, your current account balance is the direct influence of past deposits and withdrawals.

The first step in making personal-banking principles work for—not against—your marriage is for you to record and learn to understand your own personal-relationship banking history. Start by thinking through and writing down various withdrawals and deposits you remember from your younger years. What are withdrawals to you?

In my own life, a big withdrawal drained me any time someone—usually my father, later a boss—would exert excess control over me. I mentioned this earlier: I vividly recall my father and I going fishing together. If I started catching fish in one particular place, he would come over, literally shove me out of the way, and say, "Fish somewhere else."

Sadly but not surprisingly, that withdrawal from me became a pattern for how I related to others. In time I became a controlling person with my wife, and I also got in the habit of making the exact same withdrawals from my kids. This was very evident one day when we were fishing in a Colorado stream—and I was reeling them in. When all three of my kids approached with their fishing poles, I said, "No, no!"

Greg knew what I was thinking. Finally he screamed, "Dad, we are not trying to fish here! Kari broke her leg!"

With that news, for a brief second I thought, *Ohhh, I'm going to have to leave this great fishing place!* I handed Greg my pole and said, "You fish here for a while so I don't miss anything." Then I took care of Kari. Even when we're aware of the reality—the record—of our childhood withdrawals, we can still not really understand how influential they are in terms of our current practice.

So jot down some of the withdrawals drained from your emotional-relational account as you were growing up. This exercise can be useful to you in two ways:

1. It can help you to identify potential ways you are making withdrawals from your spouse's account. If a parent drained energy from you by doing x, y, and z, are you similarly draining energy from your spouse?

2. It can help you as you think through some of the things that are relational withdrawals from you today. What does your mate do that drains energy from you? Are some of these withdrawals directly connected to—triggered by—things that happened in your childhood?

As opportunities arise, share your childhood and current relational withdrawals with your mate (using "I feel" statements or word pictures, not accusations).

What energized you as a child? As a young adult? While withdrawals frequently are caused by elements beyond our control (an emotionally healthy person doesn't seek out draining withdrawals), deposits tend to be things we initiate or search out. And while withdrawals are often seen as being "done to" us, relational deposits are often things "done with" or "done for" us.

As for deposits in my own background, one of the biggest was singing with other people. Starting when I was in third grade, my sister taught me every popular song of the day, and I would harmonize with her. I got so much energy from that! Then I started singing with three or four friends. Rather than dating a lot as teens, we would go for long drives, singing on

A love that lasts forever asks for feedback.

wheels. I enjoy close harmony so much that sometimes I wonder if I should have been a singer instead of a speaker! (Then I listen to myself sing in the shower, and I know why I'm only speaking in public.)

Think through your own childhood and up through the early years of your marriage. Then write down what some of the major relational deposits have been. Again, this exercise can be useful to you as you consider how you tend to make deposits to your spouse's account. Do you "make deposits" that are more suitable to your own needs than to your spouse's? It can also help you as you think through your current-day relational deposits. What does your mate do that energizes you? Are some of these deposits directly connected to things that happened in your childhood?

As opportunity arises, discuss your deposit history and current balance with your mate.

BANKING WITH YOUR SPOUSE

The second step in using this principle involves discovering what constitutes a deposit or a withdrawal for your mate.

As you might guess from my descriptions of the first years of our marriage . . . when I eventually asked Norma to look back and reflect on those days, she was hard-pressed to think of deposits I had made. Unfortunately she had no problem remembering plenty of with-drawals. She may have been charmed with me in our courting days, but living with me was no energizing venture.

For example, because I was so much into control, her stomach would turn every time I called a family meeting. She would say with her eyes and sometimes with her words, "I hate your meetings." For the longest time, I never understood why. Then I came to learn that too much control or too much distance in relationships drains people of their energy.

Another big withdrawal for her has to do with my driving habits. She's helped me understand the seed of this negative reaction to what I perceive as perfectly passable driving skills. When Norma was in high school, she was in a major car crash with some friends. The car went over a cliff, and two of her friends were killed. Norma suffered a broken neck and was in a cast for a long time. It's perfectly reasonable that she has a healthy fear of a car going out of control. If I'm driving and get distracted and veer a bit too much toward the edge of the road, she'll say, "Oohh, you're over too far." That's a withdrawal. And if I make light of her concern and tension, that's a serious withdrawal. On the other hand, if I make a point of driving carefully, that's a big deposit.

My snoring is another major withdrawal for Norma—keeping her from getting sleep and draining energy from her. This withdrawal doesn't fit the pattern I've previously presented—

where something in childhood affects the present. Nor does it involve something I "do to" Norma. But it is something I do—or utter—that affects her negatively. And it is something one can make efforts to stop.

Of course, she had to convince me of the reality of this annoying pattern. She once recorded the sounds and played the tape back to me so I couldn't claim my "innocence." Can you imagine sleeping next to a rumbling diesel engine all those years? I've been kicked and told to roll over on my side many times, but nothing has worked so far. I've looked into new approaches to knocking out the noise. And I've just been fitted for a breathing device that completely stops my snoring, and, by the way, I have twice the energy each day.

Think back over your experience with your mate. Write down actions, attitudes, or words (or noises!) you are sure she or he perceives to be withdrawals. But then—to increase the intimacy of your conversation and to confirm your assumptions—ask your spouse whether your memories and perceptions are accurate.

When couples attending my seminars talk to each other about this, common withdrawals for women include "being treated like I don't exist," "he's never on time," and "he travels too much in his job." Common withdrawals for husbands include "she's always on my case" and "she doesn't initiate sex."

What can you do to reduce the number of withdrawals you make from your spouse's account?

MAKING A DEPOSIT TO YOUR MATE

Previously I noted that making a deposit in someone's account often involves doing something "with" or "for" someone. I've learned that for Norma, a huge deposit has to do with shopping—especially Christmas shopping. She likes to start shopping for presents in January. Now, I'm not big on shopping in the first place, and I hate to buy a present and then hide it somewhere; I want to give it to the person right away. So for the first several years of our marriage, I frustrated Norma and made big withdrawals by waiting until December 24 to do my shopping.

As we talked and I learned in this area, I came to understand that I could turn things around and make huge deposits just by changing my attitude toward shopping. So now, even though I still don't care to shop by myself, I make an effort to be enthusiastic when I'm doing it with her, whether she's buying presents or looking for a dress for herself. I try not to be like the guy who found out his wife's credit cards had been stolen, yet a year later he still hadn't reported it because the thief spent less than his wife had!

Now, for me, fishing is my shopping. If she suggests taking a picnic on the boat, I know she's saying, "I love you." She doesn't actually go fishing with me. She would rather bring a book along and read. That's okay—I just like to be with her on or near the water.

Today, Norma and I are best friends. We love finding out new things that make deposits into our accounts with each other. We go out of our way to make sure we're making more deposits than withdrawals.

A love that lasts forever says,

"Thanks. I needed that."

When I ask couples for things they consider to be deposits, common responses include "him chatting with me when he gets home from work," "daily verbal expressions of love," "it's a big deposit when she initiates sex," and "I love it when he plays with our kids." That last one is a prime example of something a man might never identify as a deposit unless he asks for feedback. My wife, too, has told me that it's a big deposit for her when I praise and encourage our kids—and especially the grandkids.

Dr. John Gottman has actually figured out through his research the ratio of deposits versus withdrawals for long-lasting, loving marriages: It's an average of five positive deposits for each negative withdrawal. In other words, at the end of a week, month, or year, the deposits should outweigh the withdrawals five to one.

Don't Rely on Guesswork

What's the best way to find out what your spouse "receives" as a withdrawal or deposit? Ask! If you're both familiar with this concept, you might say straight out as you do something with honoring intent: "I'm hoping this is a deposit with you. Does it work?" The response you get will tell you if you missed the mark or hit the bull's-eye.

If you were to ask your spouse today, "What's my balance?" what would the response be?

Whatever the answer, you can start improving your balance instantly by making deposits and by practicing self-restraint—refraining from making costly withdrawals. Do this regularly for a month or two. Then ask the question again. And watch your balance soar.

Think of this as responsible relationship banking. Practice it and reap the bountiful rewards: the pleasure of seeing your love grow stronger with every passing year—as you and your spouse walk together into the forever.

A Love That Lasts Forever

For years I've been urging people to see how much we need to help each other develop the "greatest" love. I call it heroic love—a love that sacrifices itself for the enrichment of the other, that doesn't seek its own good but chooses to satisfy the desires of the beloved.

But don't get the impression that heroic love is all self-sacrifice. From looking at my own marriage and hundreds of others, I've come to understand that enriching the life of another is often more satisfying than doing something for ourselves. As we reach out to another, our own needs for fulfillment and love are met.

I've seen that the most satisfied, joyous couples are those that have learned heroic love and practice it daily. When a husband and wife both want their partner to receive life's best before they do, they have a marriage that's going to exceed every wedding-day dream. Their love not only lasts; it continually grows.

That's the kind of relationship Charlie and Lucy Wedemeyer enjoy. If our world could raise its vision of love to their level . . . I can hardly imagine what it would be like to live on this planet.

As we reach out to another, our own

needs for fulfillment and love are met.

More than fifteen years ago, doctors diagnosed thirty-year-old Charlie Wedemeyer as having progressively debilitating and paralyzing ALS—commonly called Lou Gehrig's disease. They gave the California high-school football coach one year to live. But Charlie proved them wrong. Despite the relentless, progressive nature of his illness, he continued coaching for seven more years.

When Charlie could no longer walk, Lucy drove him up and down the sidelines in a golf cart. When he could no longer talk, she read his lips and relayed his instructions to the players. And in his dramatic last season as a coach, after he had gone on twenty-four-hour-a-day life support, his team won a state championship!

Lucy Wedemeyer is a heroic lover. She says that from the very beginning of Charlie's illness, they've focused on what they have together rather than on what they're missing. She admits it hasn't been easy, but she says in her book, *Charlie's Victory.*

"I think we communicate and understand each other better today than we ever did. While I've learned to read Charlie's lips, I find I often don't have to. His eyes almost always tell me exactly how he feels, and his eyebrows punctuate those feelings as they bounce up and down or I watch his forehead furrow into a wrinkle. And if you don't think someone in difficult circumstances can find happiness and contentment, if you doubt the contagious quality of joy, well, you've never seen Charlie smile."

When the ALS struck, the Wedemeyers had two young children and mountains of dreams they would never realize. One week after they were told of his impending death, while watching snow drift by the window of a borrowed mountain cabin, Lucy looked into Charlie's eyes and recognized the same raw emotions she felt churning inside herself. She had never felt more love

for Charlie, or more loved by him, than she did that special evening. And yet, she says, "I'd

never in my life felt such pain. Such anguish. Tears filled our eyes. Neither of us dared speak

for fear the floodgates would open. So we just sat silently, holding

hands across the table, basking in the bittersweet warmth

of that moment, wishing the romantic spell could

somehow make time stand still. All the while won-

dering how much time we had left together."

When I first met the Wedemeyers, I couldn't

help but see the radiant joy on Lucy's face and the

contentment in Charlie's eyes. They're the type of

heroes I would love to be like someday. No matter

what I go through with Norma, we both hope to have

people look into our eyes and see a similar enduring fire of love—for life and for each other.

Lucy prays daily for continued strength, because Charlie needs constant care. Some

realities of her life are harsh and ever-present, and still she says, "I wouldn't trade my life

for anyone else's. It's been so rewarding." How can she mean that? That's the beauty of

heroic love. It can move mountains, cross rivers, and overcome any obstacle for the joy set

before it. No one's life is laughing-happy every day, but people like Lucy have such a deep

sense of satisfaction and love that, no matter what occurs, they rest on an underlying assurance

that everything is still okay.

Every marriage will have its better and worse times, its springs and summers and falls and winters. Forever-love allows that full range of seasons. Enjoy the bright colors and warmth of good days. Accept the dark, rainy days, the cold of winter, and the hot summer winds of disagreement and of waiting for someone to say, "I'm sorry. I was wrong. I love you. Will you forgive me?"

With our society driven more and more by instant everything, many of us are losing the awareness that some of the best things in life take longer and aren't enjoyed until, like ripe fruit, they're ready to be picked. Charlotte, for example, came close to giving up many times with her husband, Mike. But if she had, it would have been too soon.

Mike, like me, didn't know how to love his wife in a way that made her feel loved. He and I struggled through many seasons—many ups and downs—together as we learned the things I teach in this book. And as he grew in his own happiness and in his sensitivity to her needs, she found herself in the kind of relationship she had dreamed about before they married.

Not long ago I got a letter from Charlotte. "I never thought the day would come," she said, "when my life with Mike would be so wonderful. As you know, we've had our 'down times.' But this last year has been worth all we went through. Whatever we didn't have before has long since been forgotten because of what we have today."

Unfortunately, many couples don't wait for that exciting season that wipes out the memory of the difficult times. That good season is like picking delicious fruit after a hard winter, wet spring, and hot summer. The juicy apples need all three seasons to taste delightfully good.

But many other couples have come to realize that it's perfectly normal for a marriage to go through different seasons—of drought, worry, sadness, anger, and also times of plenty, happiness, and overwhelming joy and laughter.

Whatever season you are in today as you begin your marriage or as you look back on and forward to years of marriage, what I wish most for you is a lifetime spent learning more about loving each other well. I hope that yours will be an enduring love as you face the future together and that you'll create together a love that truly lasts forever.

Don't miss these other enriching products by

relationship expert Gary Smalley

The Hidden Value of a Man (audio cassette)

The Incredible Worth of a Woman (video)

The Key to Your Child's Heart

Love Is a Decision

Making Love Last Forever (book and video)

Seven Promises Practiced,
Video 4: *A Man and His Family*

About the Author

One of the foremost experts on family relationships, Dr. Gary Smalley has written numerous best-selling, award-winning books, based on more than thirty years experience as a teacher and counselor. He has appeared on hundreds of local and national radio and television programs. Smalley and his wife of thirty-five years, Norma, reside in Branson, Missouri.